SHITHOLE
Countries

Donald Gorbach

ISBN-10 1983864684
ISBN-13 978-1983864681

"WHY WOULD KIM JUNG-UN INSULT ME
BY CALLING ME 'OLD' WHEN I WOULD NEVER
CALL HIM 'SHORT AND FAT.'
OH WELL, I TRY SO HARD TO BE HIS FRIEND…"

—DONALD TRUMP

REALITYCOVERBOOKS.COM

African Nations

El Salvador

Haiti

* 9 7 8 1 9 8 3 8 6 4 6 8 1 *